DRAGON TALK

Fleur Adcock was born in New Zealand in 1934. She spent the war years in England, returning with her family to New Zealand in 1947. She emigrated to Britain in 1963, working as a librarian in London until 1979. In 1977-78 she was writer-in-residence at Charlotte Mason College of Education, Ambleside. She was Northern Arts Literary Fellow in 1979-81, living in Newcastle, becoming a freelance writer after her return to London. She received an OBE in 1996, and the Queen's Gold Medal for Poetry in 2006 for *Poems 1960-2000* (Bloodaxe Books, 2000).

Fleur Adcock published three pamphlets with Bloodaxe: *Below Loughrigg* (1979), *Hotspur* (1986) and *Meeting the Comet* (1988), as well as her translations of medieval Latin lyrics, *The Virgin & the Nightingale* (1983). All her other collections were published by Oxford University Press until they shut down their poetry list in 1999, after which Bloodaxe published her collected poems, *Poems 1960-2000* (2000), followed by ten years later by *Dragon Talk* (2010).

FLEUR ADCOCK

DRAGON TALK

BLOODAXE BOOKS

ISBN: 978 1 85224 878 9

First published 2010 by
Bloodaxe Books Ltd,
Highgreen,
Tarset,
Northumberland NE48 1RP.

www.bloodaxebooks.com
For further information about Bloodaxe titles
please visit our website or write to
the above address for a catalogue.

Supported by
**ARTS COUNCIL
ENGLAND**

Cover design: Neil Astley & Pamela Robertson-Pearce.

Printed in Great Britain by
Bell & Bain Limited, Glasgow, Scotland.

To the memory of my mother
Irene Adcock, née Robinson
(1908-2001)

ACKNOWLEDGEMENTS

Acknowledgements are due to the editors of the following publications in which some of these poems first appeared: *Agenda*, *Ambit*, *NZSA Bulletin of New Zealand Studies*, *PN Review*, *Poetry Review*, *The Rialto*, *The Spectator*, *The Times Literary Supplement* and *Thumbscrew*. Parts of the sequence now entitled 'My First Twenty Years' were published in *PN Review* under the title 'My English Childhood'. 'Fast Forward' was one of a group of three poems commissioned by Philip Lewis to celebrate his wife Linda's 70th birthday.

CONTENTS

Dragon Talk

How many years ago now
did we first walk hand in hand –
or hand in claw –
through Alice's Wonderland,

your favourite training ground,
peopled with a crew
of phantasms – Mock Turtle, Gryphon –
as verbal as you?

Your microphone, kissing my lips,
inhaled my words; the machine
displayed them, printed out
in sentences on a screen.

*

My codependant,
my precious parasite,
my echo, my parrot,
my tolerant slave:

I do the talking;
you do the typing.
Just try a bit harder
to hear what I say!

I wait for you to lash your tail
each time I swear at you.
But no: you listen meekly,
and print 'fucking moron'.

*

All the come-ons
you transcribed as commas –
how can we conduct a flirtation
in punctuation? –

Particularly when,
money-mad creature,
you spell doom to romance
by writing 'flotation'.

*

I can't blame you for homonyms,
but surely after a decade
you could manage the last word
of Cherry Tree 'Would'?

Context, after all,
is supposed to be your engine.
Or are you being driven
by Humpty Dumpty?

*

I take it amiss
when you mis-hear the names
of my nearest and dearest;
in particular, Beth.

Safer, perhaps, if I say Bethany.
Keep your scary talons
off my great-granddaughter:
don't call her 'death'.

*

You know all the diseases
and the pharmaceuticals:
bronchopneumonia,
chloramphenicol

are no trouble to you,
compulsive speller,
hypochondriac,
virtual dealer.

*

You're hopeless at birds:
can't get wren into your head –
too tiny, you try to tell me:
it comes out as rain or ring.

Let's try again: blackbird, osprey,
hen, (much better), kingfisher, hawk,
duckling. But I have to give up
and type Jemima Puddleduck.

*

What am I thinking of,
dragon bird?
How could I forget
that you too have wings?

Fly to me;
let me nuzzle your snout,
whisper orders, trust you
to carry them out.

*

Do I think of you as 'he'? –
Beyond male or female;
utterly alien,
yet as close as my breath –

invisible, intangible,
you hover at my lips –
am I going too far?
Are we into theology?

*

Animal, vegetable or mineral?
Who's playing these games? –
Abstract, with mineral connections
and a snazzy coat of scales.

Gentle dragon, stupid beast,
why do I tease you?
Laughter's not in your vocabulary:
all you understand are words.

*

Today I saw you cresting the gable
of someone's roof: a curly monster
smaller than me, but far too large
to hide yourself inside a computer.

They'd painted you red – was that your choice?
But this was only your graven image.
Your private self was at home, waiting
for reincarnation through my voice.

12

MY FIRST TWENTY YEARS

Kuaotunu

This is the schoolhouse at Kuaotunu,
on the hill, with Daddy's school next door,

and this is my little red watering-can;
I've just been splashing some dirt with it.

In the kitchen is Jammy Jean,
washing the dishes; Mummy's sitting

on the verandah, feeding the baby.
I'm the big sister now; I'm two.

The fireguard is made of blackboard
for me to chalk on. I'm drawing a face.

Inside my head I can see it clearly,
but my fingers won't do what I tell them.

It turns out to be a round patch
of scribble. It looks more like the world.

Linseed

The knees I'm embracing through her skirt
are Grandma Robinson's; above them
is a dark blue jumper, a bit scratchy.

I can just reach it. I must be three.
She's trying to sweep the kitchen floor,
and I'm tripping her up. She's not cross yet.

There's some linseed boiling on the stove –
tiny brown jellies, with seeds in them.
I can't be expected to know what for.

The milk she squeezes out of the cow
turns into butter when she churns it.
Life's mysterious, but I'm used to that.

Illiterate

That gaping boredom before I learned to read –
sitting on the sheepskin rug, wailing
'Mummy, I don't know what to do!'

(The baby asleep, no one to play with,
no kindergarten until the morning,
and no idea when the afternoon would end.)

'Why don't you do some colouring in?' she'd say.
'Here are the crayons' – except I thought she called them
'crowns', like what the King wore on his head.

It was sometimes hard to get a grip on words.
That snail bread, for example: I watched her slice it,
waiting for the knife to expose a shell.

There was always something new to puzzle out,
and old stuff to unlearn (the singular
of matches, it turned out, was match, not 'matcher').

Thank God Chicken Licken came along,
a year or two later, to rescue me.
Life makes a lot more sense when you can spell.

Food

Spanish cream, cloudy with beaten egg-white,
standing in a cold bath until it jells;
stewed prunes in a bowl in the pantry;

butter in the safe, except for some
left on the table; I climb on a chair
and am caught raiding it. (I like salt.)

My favourite meal is mashed potatoes,
with gravy or with a buried treasure
of butter to find. I don't mind cabbage.

Once, as an experiment, I bite off
a chip of apple and ram it up my nose.
What pain, until it shrivels and falls out!

And yet how superior I feel
coming in from the sandpit to report
'Mummy, Baby's eating sand again.'

Lollies

The only chocolate I still like
is crisp and dark as the shards of Easter egg
my father shared with me when I was four

outside in the caravan: a treat
to keep me quiet, and avoid disturbing
the household so early in the morning.

We were not brought up to eat sweets.
'If someone offers you lollies,' they told us,
'say no, thank you, they're bad for my teeth.'

Little prigs, we obeyed at first.
Only later, in England, did they relent –
if something's rationed, you must be allowed it.

But back there in pre-war New Zealand
sweets were medicinal: barley sugar
if you felt sick in the Baby Austin,

or for me, after the surgeon
had scraped the flesh off my poisoned finger,
bribes to let my mother change the dressing:

a choice of pastel-coloured cachous –
mauve, pink, pale-green or lemon – powdery
and perfumed like a handkerchief sachet.

Rangiwahia

When the kitten got its head stuck
in a cream-jug Mummy ran across
to a plumber laying drains next door
at the school. He slid his tin-clippers

beween the enamel neck of the jug
and the soft, furry neck inside.
Out shot the kitten, up a drainpipe
and into our memories for life.

The other scene presented to me
for my retention was the earthquake.
It made the playground ripple, they said,
pointing out into the dark.

But I was too sleepy, snatched from bed
and clutched under a safe doorframe;
my focus wouldn't open out
further than their wondering faces.

My own chief marker for the place
was nothing visual; it was the wind
moaning in the telegraph wires
as I hung swinging on the gate –

bored, waiting for Daddy to come
from the school for tea; hearing the sky:
the loneliest music in all the world.
How could air make you feel so sad?

Drury Goodbyes

What with getting in the way of the packing
and not being allowed to go to
the big event, Great-granny's funeral,

we found something silly to do, and did it:
we sat the new dolls on the potty
after we'd done wees in it ourselves.

Next day we were going away in a boat
so big that you could stand up in it,
they said, and it wouldn't tip over.

There was no time to dry the soggy dolls;
they were left behind – all but my Margaret,
who wouldn't bend enough to dunk her bottom.

3 September 1939

Hindsight says we were in the Red Sea,
heading for Suez. Late afternoon;

sultry, I guess. I woke up half dazed
to a flurry in the darkish cabin:

that being-late feeling, Mummy in a rush.
She trotted us to the empty dining-room.

'We fell asleep and missed the children's dinner,'
she said. They rustled up a meal for us –

turkey minced in some kind of sauce –
as they told her 'That's not all you missed.'

A fricassee, I think, is what you'd call it.

Sidcup, 1940

I was writing my doll's name on the back of her neck
when Mummy caught fire — a noisy distraction.

She was wearing a loose blue flowered smock
(an old maternity smock, I now deduce,

from her pregnancy with my sister four years earlier,
being used as an overall, not to waste it);

the hem flapped over the hearth she was sweeping,
and caught on a live coal from last night's fire.

I tore myself away from writing 'Margaret'
to save her life. 'Lie down, Mummy!' I said,

and helped to smother her flames in the hearthrug.
So much is memory. The rest was praise:

What a good girl, how sensible, how calm!
But 'how well-taught' is what they should have said.

She saved her own life, really. She'd made sure
we knew fire travels upwards, and needs air.

After all, this was the 'phoney war' –
she was waiting for all of England to catch fire.

My First Letter

Dear Mammy [Auntie's spelling, I suspect:
a Leicestershire phonetic transcription
from my still slightly New Zealand accent,
soon to be lost]. *We sat on the platform
three times last Sunday. We did like it.
We go to school. We like to go to school.*

That's all, apart from half a page of kisses
and a rather fine drawing on the other side.

What was it we liked, then, exactly?
Sunday School? Did sitting on the platform
make us important? We certainly liked school –
or I did; Marilyn was not so keen,
but she was only four. And we liked the farm,
and our new Auntie and Uncle, and Betty and Jean.

We liked Mummy, too – and Daddy, of course –
but they weren't there. You can't have everything.

Ambulance Attendant

What happened to that snapshot of my mother
in her grey Ambulance Service overcoat

and a tin hat, her gas-mask hanging
from a diagonal strap across her chest?

It wasn't flattering. She may have burnt it,
out of vanity. Too late: I can still see it.

All she ever told us about that year
was the tale of how they parked over a time-bomb –

unscathed, of course; a big joke, afterwards.
But the picture grows clearer by the minute:

the double row of buttons; the pockets;
the collar; her determined chin.

Off Duty at the Depot

There stands my father in ARP overalls
with his arm around a plump blonde lady.
They are both holding tennis racquets;
their heads are tilted towards each other.

Who took the photo? Some colleague of theirs,
no doubt – you can see the depot behind them.
Not my mother. But 'Auntie Joan'
ripened into a friend of the family.

Later, when I was eleven or so,
she came with presents for Christmas. Mine
was *The Rubaiyat of Omar Khayyam*.
I found it totally seductive.

Just in Case

'If anything happens to us,' they said,
sitting down with us at the farmhouse table
on one of their rare visits from the Blitz –

'it won't, of course – don't worry – but if it did
you'd go back to live in New Zealand
with Auntie Alma'.
                    Why Auntie Alma?

Couldn't we go to Grandma and Uncle Len
and Auntie Cynthia and Rose and Don?
Couldn't we just stay here?
                    Apparently not;

it was Auntie Alma with her rimless glasses
and Uncle Leslie and his stamp collection.
What a good thing nothing happened!

Fake Fur

Instead of a teddy there was Bobby, my dog.
I hugged him bald, and his legs went wobbly:
you could see the folded straw inside the cloth.

Later, when I could sew, I covered him
in white satin, trimly stitched to fit,
with black velvet for the perky terrier tail:

perfect, up to the shoulders – at which point
my creativity failed. But the eyes, I thought,
serene in the threadbare face, forgave me.

A Rose Tree

When we went to live at Top Lodge
my mother gave me a rose tree.

She didn't have to pay for it –
it was growing there already,

tall and old, by the gravel drive
where we used to ride our scooters.

No one else was allowed to pick
the huge pale blooms that smelt like jam.

It was mine all through that summer.
In October we moved again.

But even never seeing it
couldn't stop it from being mine:

one of those eternal presents.
At the new house I had a duck.

Glass

On the bus, you added up the numbers
on your ticket: if they came to 21
that meant you were going to get a sweetheart.

But if you walked to school, you might be able
to add to your collection of coloured glass:
rubies and sapphires; bits of saints and martyrs.

Casein

The knife handles were made out of milk,
my mother said: like cheese. I thought of the skin
on cocoa, and had to believe her;
the handles looked creamy, after all.

But when it came to buttons, that was harder;
and knitting-needles – so many colours,
and that smooth, clicky feel against your teeth
when you tapped them: all made out of milk.

Teeth were quite interesting, too.

Glitterwax

That winter's craze, in 1943:
slabs of the greenest green, the frostiest white,
all colours the most intense and shiny.

You warmed them in your hands, and genius flowered.
I fashioned a perfect snowdrop, on a stiff wire –
bell cup, green dots. You could mould anything.

It was the apotheosis of modelling clay:
silky as poison, the plasticine of the gods.
Yet the world has decided to live without it.

Bananas

The first banana I'd seen for years
was at school assembly, tenderly swaddled
in cotton wool. Someone's father

had brought it home on leave with him.
The raffle tickets were 6d each,
for the Red Cross. I forget who won it.

The next was sliced and drowning in custard –
'Auntie' Lena's way of stretching it.
Sacrilege. But then this was a woman

whose husband left his clothes by a river
to get away. (A dozen years later
he popped up alive, and she took him back.)

Not that I knew all this at the time;
but even before the banana, you could
tell by her corsets she had no taste.

Clay

Just before we left the farm by the brickworks
Peter Jackson smashed my clay tea-set,
thus ensuring that I'd remember him for ever.

Each lumpy cup, saucer, jug, plate or bowl
I'd fashioned out of the beige-blue squelchiness
had taken days to bake hard in the sun.

No time to make more; our holiday was over.
My mother, coming to collect us, said:
'It will all be the same in a hundred years'.

I quoted it back at her after the first fifty –
still unconsoled. But now, too late to tell her,
I give in. So it will, Mother. Clay crumbles.

The Mill Stream

And what was the happiest day I remember?
It was when we went to the Mill Stream –

my sister and I and the Morris kids.
We wore our bathing-suits under our dresses

(subterfuge), crossed the live railway lines
(forbidden), and tramped through bluebell woods.

There was a bridge with green and brown shadows
to lurk among in the long afternoon.

Chest high in the stream, with pointy water-snails
as escorts, I could hardly believe my luck.

Happiness is chemical. Sunshine and water
trigger it. (And I couldn't even swim.)

Morrison Shelter

Marilyn was frightened of snakes, mostly –
quite convinced a boa-constrictor lurked

under the eiderdown, or perhaps just
a nest of adders. I was full of scorn:

even real snakes didn't bother me –
and how could they have got into her bed?

My own nightmares (fewer – I was older)
were about ghosts: doors couldn't keep those out.

Oddly enough, being in bed with Mummy –
that outgrown childhood remedy – did the trick.

It also worked for pythons in the blankets.
So when we all slept in the table shelter

nobody woke up screaming. After all,
being scared of bombs was just for grown-ups.

Direct Hit

I

The way they told it to us at the time,
if he hadn't swapped his day off with a friend
to come home for his birthday, he'd have been killed.

But the friend, unlike our father, was not a driver,
and therefore hadn't run to where the cars were
when he heard the siren, and was thus not killed.

So that was all right, or not so bad – until
you thought about it, which they hoped we wouldn't:
somebody had to run and start the cars.

II

The way he told his parents, two weeks later:
'Times have been quite exciting. Fortunately
I still have my lucky star and am safe and sound.

Our depot, however, was completely demolished,
which explains why this letter is not typed...
I have lost both my cars but they will be covered

by war damage insurance...' Typewriter? Cars?
No word of people? – Not while it's still going on.
But on the day after his next birthday,

June 1945, one sentence:
'Just a year ago today I was helping
to dig my friends from the debris of the depot'.

III

So who was killed? They're in the *Kentish Times*
('FLYING BOMBS HIT SOUTHERN ENGLAND.
First-Aid and Rescue Service Depot Destroyed'):

Mrs W. Symes; Miss L. Hancock;
Mr B. Hopwell; Mr E. Ingram;
Mr Norman White; and a messenger named Smith.

Mr Dolman

My mother, dusting Mr Dolman's parlour
in the winter of 1944,

misplaced one of his Staffordshire dogs
by an inch or two. 'Oi keeps ee *thur!*'

the old man snarled, as he moved it back.
Thirty years later, 'Oi keeps ee thur',

I'd say to my son as he searched for something.
Thirty more years, and the Wiltshire burr

resounds again in Andrew's own house,
away in a different hemisphere –

washing the dishes, I hold up a jug:
'Where does this go?' 'Oi keeps ee thur'.

Do his daughters think of it as merely
something Dad says, or will they confer

another generation of currency
on a soundbite uttered they don't know where

by someone their grandmother's family lodged with
for a month or two in the Second World War?

Tunbridge Wells Girls' Grammar

Even snow not being what it was,
the crumbly stuff they grant us nowadays
can't match the shapely stars that hypnotised me

as they posed on my navy woollen coat-sleeves
for long enough to distract me from caring
whether or not they made me late for school.

Frant

Bliss cottage, in retrospect:
woods just across the road, a duckpond
in the field behind, cowslips...

even at the time we loved it.
Living in Sussex, going to school in Kent:
how travelled we sounded!

I had my eleventh birthday there:
books, and cake for tea in the back parlour
we rented from Mrs Gain.

We all used the big kitchen
with the range whose lid she lifted one day
when Stanley Gain (about my age,

but a boy, unfortunately)
came in dangling from a long stick something
murkily white with loops at each end:

'What's this, Mum?' 'I don't know; give it here' –
into the sizzling coals. He smirked and left.
She clanked the lid, and honoured me

with a complicit glance, as if
I were old enough to use things like that
or know what name she'd call them by.

Biro

Always one for a new invention, my father
was much taken with the clever device
he brought home to show us, early that spring:

a ballpoint pen. Where did he get it?
It was 1945. You couldn't buy one.
But the RAF were issued with them

for use at high altitudes – or so I read now.
He used to lecture to forces personnel
in the south of England. Case solved – I think.

Woodside Way

'When are we going back to Woodside Way?'
No answer; or 'Not just yet; we'll have to see.'

We couldn't make them grasp how much it mattered:
a quarter or so of our lives in one place –

and one with actual woods at the end of the road
to make free with, and friends living nearby.

It was as if a few Doodlebug raids
had jolted them into forgetting the word 'home'.

We'd moved to Scalford, Corsham, Chippenham, Frant,
and finally (a name from the past) Sidcup –

five changes of school in less than a year –
before they confessed· we had a new home now.

Woodside Way went on without us. Our friends
had other friends. New people lived in our house.

Surely they could at least have taken us back –
one little outing by train – to say goodbye

to the Morrises, and Edna and Diana
and the others, and the house itself, and the woods,

and the field beside them, ploughed for victory
each year, and Middle Bush, where the owl roosted?

Sidcup Again

Had we become suddenly posh, then, living
in this enormous house in Hatherley Road
with three storeys, rambling cellars, outbuildings,
and a garden that was an orchard as well?

Not quite. There were also Mr and Mrs Ash,
and Miss Miller, and Mr and Mrs Curtiss
and Mr Ferris – all at the same time –
and others now and then to be squeezed in.

We never knew where we'd be sleeping next:
upstairs at the back, downstairs at the front,
or al fresco in the coach house or stables
(roofed, it's true, but each of them short of a wall).

One winter our parents took to the cellar.
It was the kind of thing New Zealanders did –
unlike the Burtonshaws across the road;
nobody else lived in their house but them.

My sister and I were fond of Miss Miller
(a teacher), and the Curtisses were friendly.
They invited us to tea; we had shrimps
for the first time, and played with the baby.

Mr Ferris, who was a friend of theirs,
had a thin moustache, and looked like a spiv.
One evening he and Mr Curtiss fell out
and tumbled down the stairs in a violent clinch.

I didn't see the gun they were grappling over –
my mother screamed at me to stay in my room –
but I heard the police arrive. (Poor Marilyn
was asleep, and missed it all). No one was shot.

Mr Curtiss's thumb was broken. Mr Ferris
crawled on the floor to search for his gold tooth.
A bit of an anti-climax. Still, it was all
quite fun. I hope the Burtonshaws were jealous.

August 1945

After queueing sixteen hours for tickets
he brought us to the land beyond the war.

In Donegal he came in with a newspaper.
'They've split the atom!' And then he explained.

When VJ Day happened we were in Dublin.
Our landlady gave us some kindly advice:

'Best not to wear red, white and blue rosettes –
they might get torn off, and your lapels with them.'

Even so, when we went to the pictures –
'The Commandos Strike at Dawn' – and the camp guards

hoisted the swastika, we still couldn't quite
believe our ears when the audience cheered.

Signature

It was not sensible to write my name
by dragging my feet through the ankle-deep snow
on the playing-field – it clotted in my shoes
and short white socks. Think of the chilblains!

But I was thirteen, and sensible only
intermittently; and this famous winter –
arctic, rattling with icicles – was my last
in England; and I didn't want to leave.

On the *SS Arawa*

Torn away from England at thirteen,
like Juliet from Romeo, I dreamed
a plane swooped on the deck to whisk me back.
No chance. I had to look for distractions.

I read the entire Bible at a gallop
in five weeks (skipping the minor prophets).
I learned to swim. I wrote a comic play,
and we put it on (tickets a penny).

I found an actual Romeo, a steward,
to moon over. One night the other kids
persuaded him to kiss me, while they giggled:
not ideal, but something for my diary.

That was the kind of stuff it flourished on,
together with our exotic ports of call –
Curaçao, with bananas galore
and Dutch currency; polyglot Panama.

The doll I made for Marilyn from a pair
of pink knickers featured; and our quarrels.
I didn't mention (though I still remember)
what songs the crew's accordion used to play

on the afterdeck, those tropical evenings;
or the green-black sea and the tempting rail;
or how, in spite of Louie's Italian eyes,
my dreams were still of Surrey, Wiltshire, Sidcup.

Unrationed

I

My diary of our holiday in Ireland
is full of references to being sick.

It also describes a series of breakfasts:
eggs, bacon, fried bread, brown bread with real butter –

more grease in one meal than our weekly ration.
You'd think I might have made the connection.

II

'Legs like pea-sticks,' the aunties complained,
welcoming us home from austerity
with bulging tea-trolleys of cream sponges.

'We'll fatten you up.' Cream, butter, cheese:
New Zealand's dairy industry set to –
and failed. Fat legs were not my destiny.

The Table

What they should have taken back to New Zealand
was the oval walnut dining-table

picked up for almost nothing during the Blitz
when antiques were no one's priority:

the smoothest, most colourfully-grained,
prettiest slab of wood we ever ate off.

Once or twice, when the Doodlebugs came,
we even slept with our heads under it,

before our Morrison shelter was delivered.
But no; they took the piano instead.

It was her choice (although the table had been
hers too: her lucky find, her gleeful purchase;

he was far too busy to go shopping,
and only home on leave one night a week).

Was she trying to say she was the person
who, for a couple of years during a lull,

had a plate beside her door with letters on it
(LTCL, LRSM, etc),

and not just a furnisher of tables?
But New Zealand was full of pianos.

Back from the War

A bit over the top, I thought, the lectern
my grandfather presented to the church

(St John's, Drury – proud of its bullet-holes
from what we could still then call the Maori Wars):

'A thank-offering from Mr and Mrs S. Adcock
for the safe return of their son...and family...'

After all, we hadn't been to the front.
A few air raids, and none that struck home, were all.

Bad enough when Grandpa, standing beside me
in the pew, decided to sing falsetto.

Now here I was, implicitly included
('and family') in his embarrassing monument.

Well, I grew up. And it's gone now, the lectern –
replaced by a brass eagle, though the plaque survives.

A pity; I'd have liked another look at it.
I rather suspect the dear man made it himself.

Temporary

Adelaide Road was not a good address –
we didn't mention it at our new schools –
but it appealed to our taste for squalor.

Poverty was romantic. Was this it?
The cabin trunk we ate off, seated on boxes,
would suggest so, and the bare floorboards.

Sausage curry with potatoes and carrots,
our staple dish (though our mother afterwards
always denied it) seemed appropriate too.

My sister even relished the hot whiffs
of toffee or peppermint oozing up
from the sweet factory downstairs.

Our parents had a bed. We had inflatable
army surplus lilos, joined-up tubes
of smelly rubber with lives of their own.

It was easy to slip off on to the floor
where Marilyn's dolls were ranged for their schooling,
ready to lose their English accents.

Strangers on a Tram

I was on a tram going home from school
when who should get on it but my mother,
wearing the brown tweed costume Mrs Dowle
passed on to her before we left England.

This wouldn't have been so bad except that
she'd let the hem down because Mrs D.
had said skirts were going to be longer.
Well, if so New Zealand had not yet heard.

Mothers were supposed to be stout, with grey hair,
and not go around predicting the New Look.
There were some girls on the tram I sort of knew.
I pretended this woman was a stranger.

Amazingly, she pretended the same
(apart from giving me a furtive wink).
How dare she have the cheek to understand me!
It was hard to work out what to resent.

Her First Ball

For the school dance I wore a circular skirt –
full length, and a full-circle swirl of apple green;
I bought the pattern; my mother made the frock.

But what to do with my hair: so little-girlish,
too long? Auntie Phil came up with a green snood
and an Alice-band on which (her brainwave)

she pinned sprigs of daphne – most waxen-petalled,
extravagantly-scented of real flowers,
from the bush by our door – to intoxicate,

as it turned out, my classmate Dell's very tall
brother Ken, who danced with me all evening,
his nose hovering above the honeyed wafts.

After my friends' lunchtime coaching in the gym
I managed the quicksteps and foxtrots all right,
even in gold sandals (we all wore gold sandals).

As for underneath, I'd been given no option:
Phil and my mother had tracked down in some shop
a pair of kneelength, scratchy woollen drawers

to protect my kidneys from chills, they insisted.
I was too naive to see at the time
what it was they really wanted to guard.

Precautions

I sat on the stairs and fiddled with something
as my mother braved the pre-wedding chat:

it seemed you wrote to a doctor in Christchurch
who would send supplies under plain cover,

and – well, that was it. Struck dumb by the notion
of parental sex, I asked no questions.

We never wrote to the dubious doctor,
nor did Alistair slink into chemists' shops.

In fact we did nothing much at all;
and only after my first baby,

when my GP decided to fit me
with a diaphragm, and explained what it was,

did I get the point of my friend's grim saga
about her trek from doctor to doctor

before her wedding, being turned away
as immoral, until she found the one

who slashed her hymen with surgical scissors –
she haemorrhaged all over the couch.

At least we hadn't had that problem.

NEXT

Miramar

Miramar? No, surely not – it can't be:
the cream, clinker-built walls, the pepper tree,
the swan-plants under my bedroom window…
But if it is, I'll open the back door
to the sun porch, with its tang of baked wood.

You'll be lying propped on the shabby couch,
writing; you won't be pleased to see me,
home from school already, with my panama
and my teenage grumps, though you'll pretend
you're a gracious mother, and I a loving daughter.

After the chiropractor's fixed your back
and growing up improved my temper,
we'll learn to be good friends for forty years,
most of them spent apart, vocal with letters:
glad of each other, over all the distances –

until this one, that telescopes your past,
compacting the whole time from postwar England
to your present house into a flattened slice
of Lethe; tidily deleting my teens
from your tangled brain; obliterating Miramar.

Summer Pudding

Dare I assume I'll remember the summer pudding
I made last week with a heap of mixed berries
and shiny red currants? It was the first for years.

My mother used to make them during the war
from hedgerow blackberries and the sugar ration,
saved for the purpose, with top-of-the-milk for cream.

And then she forgot. Not just the occasions,
but the method – the bread-lined basin, the small plate
for a lid, with a weight on it; the lot.

She came across the recipe, when she was old,
and announced 'I've made my first summer pudding'.
It was to be for Christmas, the following week.

But she'd made it too early. It sat in the fridge
getting soggier and more slimy. When the day came
we ate it, to please her. It was disgusting.

Lost

She is prowling around the flat
all night, looking for the children.

Her granddaughter comes and tells her
they are safely tucked up in bed.

'No, not your children,' she says, 'mine.
Where can they be? I can't find them.'

By daylight she finds us often:
two grown women, in our sixties.

Only in her dreams are we lost,
as sometimes she was lost in ours.

But what if we had found her then,
when we were still her little girls –

woken up in the night and found
a 90-year-old great-granny

crying out in our mother's voice,
and no mother to comfort us?

That Butterfly

(i.m. Irene Adcock, 1908-2001)

It's true about the butterfly –
a peacock, no common tortoiseshell –
that surged in through my open window.

You were in your coffin in New Zealand.
I was here, in my hot London study,
trying to get my voice to work

as Marilyn held the telephone
over your dead face. You couldn't wait:
you fluttered in at once to comfort me.

You were no showy beauty, dear mother,
but your personality was bright rainbow,
and your kindness had velvety wings.

An Observation

Walking about from room to room
to find the source of all this moonlight
I notice I can still remember
the rules for the declension of adjectives
after the article in German:
'der volle Mond; ein voller Mond' –

and there it is, in front of the house,
not even halfway around it yet
but shining full and flat into my eyes;
which means it can't be as late as I thought
(not much past 3 A.M., it turns out);
and I am still a day off 70.

Outside the Crematorium

Flirting with death, after my third funeral
in a month, I chat with the undertaker,
a dashing figure in his designer beard
and frock-coat. He was at school with my son.

They used to play in his father's workshop.
'One day I'll come here in my coffin,'
I tell him. 'I'd like you to see me off.
Andrew will arrange it. How's the family?'

The last stragglers have viewed the flowers
and are drifting towards their cars. The vicar
has apologised to me for the 'poem'
he read with such professional gravity.

Some of my neighbours are walking home –
Peggy was local (the pet-shop lady).
The sun is shining calmly. I could almost
get used to this death business – except

that our last funeral was for a baby,
whose grandmother has just been telling us
how she helped to wash and dress her for it,
and how hard it was to get her vest on.

A Petition

Lord, let me learn to love
the pumping station at the edge of the wood
where the wild arum lilies grew.

Help me to welcome loft extensions,
and in particular the one replacing
the roof where the housemartins always nested.

Teach me the charms of the neighbours' cat
who slaughtered our thrushes, widowed the robin,
and wiped out all the dunnocks, one by one.

Convince me that a hedge of Leylandii
and some grass are better for the frogs
than the pond that seethed with tadpoles every spring.

Make me a devotee of Health and Safety,
hostile to trees (you never know,
their branches might fall off on someone).

Let concrete be my favourite colour,
and petrol fumes my drug of choice,
that I may live happy in my skin.

To the Robins

Innocent receptacles of my love
which I convey in the form of mealworms
when I can get them, or at other times
disguised as tiny morsels of cheese,

I gaze into your eyes, one at a time,
and you gaze back, trying to predict me,
lurking hopefully on the windowsill
but ready to fly if I turn nasty.

Your love is only for each other.
It is embodied mostly in food;
what you really like is 'courtship feeding' –
beak to beak, as if posing for 'Springwatch'.

When he jumped on you (at this point the pronoun
bifurcates from dual to singular),
my fellow female, he was off in a second.
You quivered with astonishment for minutes.

You definitely preferred the foreplay –
the chocolates and champagne, as it were;
in view of which, accept my platonic
offering: a bowl of little wrigglers.

A Garland for Rosa

Skype

More technology, and it brings me Rosa,
captured in mid-scamper by a parent
to wave hello to her London grandma.

'Baby,' she says, in an almost French accent –
the pure vowels of the novice talker,
although she's a New Zealand child: 'Bébé!'

What she sees is her miniaturised self
in the lower left hand corner of the screen;
and in the centre, wistfully beaming, me:

to whom she's half blowing a kiss – it's planted
on her hand, but she forgets to throw it;
and I can't quite reach to it through the glass.

Rosa Mundi

Dear Rosa, twenty years before I knew
that one day there might be someone like you
I planted this: a rose with which you share
part of your name – as also with 'the Fair
Rosamund'; the rose of the world, it means.
The colours are pinks, whites, reds and in-betweens,
all mingled. Roses come in many types,
but how could I resist one that has stripes? –
a bit like Milly-Molly-Mandy's dress
and a bit like a long-ago princess.
You'll see it one day. But although I'm fond
of the rose, you might prefer what's in the pond
beside it, flicking its slender tail: a newt,
a miniature dragon. What could be more cute?

Fenlanders

These are the fens.
And suddenly I half expect

the ghosts of your local ancestors
to flap up, hooting,

out of the black soil
some of them helped to drain.

How will they be disguised?
Geese, will they be? Snipe, mallards?

Two centuries ago
when all this was water

they were hatched around here.
Their very names have wings:

Samuel Spinks and his grandmothers
Anne Bird and Elizabeth Sparrow.

(I am not making this up,
and you are too young to think it odd.)

Perhaps they'll waddle in
kitted out in bills and feathers

with fluffy, strokeable breasts.
Would you like that, my little ducky?

Fast Forward

Holding the photograph of Mary Ellen,
my great-grandmother the midwife,
to gaze more closely at her face,
I see on my desk behind the frame
another picture, in another frame:
my blonde granddaughter holding her baby.
They are standing in a doorway,
just off to a lecture on *Beowulf.*

Suddenly a rushing of wings
as the generations between accelerate
like a fan of pages riffling over
or like the frames that rattled past
as I swooped into the anaesthetic
for my tonsillectomy, when I was nine.
Face after face, all with our imprint,
humming forwards. We can do anything.